Written by
ANNA CLAYBOURNE

SKYGAZING

Illustrated by
KERRY HYNDMAN

WELBECK
EDITIONS

Published in 2021 by Welbeck Editions

An imprint of Welbeck Children's Limited,

part of Welbeck Publishing Group.

20 Mortimer Street, London W1T 3JW

Design Manager: Emily Clarke

Designer: Ceri Hurst

Associate Publisher: Laura Knowles

Editor: Jenni Lazell

A CIP catalogue record for this book is available from the British Library.

ISBN 978-1-91351-903-2

Printed in Heshan, China

10 9 8 7 6 5 4 3 2 1

CONTENTS

Day begins

Every morning, the Sun rises, filling the vast, wide sky with light. Wherever you go, the sky surrounds you: endless and always changing — from the piercing bright blue of a summer day, to cloud-studded, pink and orange at sunset, or thunderous dark charcoal before a storm.

The sky can blind you with light, wash you with rain, or sprinkle you with snow. It's the domain of swooping birds, migrating butterflies, hot-air balloons and helicopters, sudden lightning, and shimmering rainbows.

Look up, and you can feel how tiny you are. It's a sight that links you with everyone and everything on the planet, as we all share the same sky.

Bright skies

If you lie on the grass on a sunny day, and look up...
you see the sky, like a huge, smooth, bright blue
dome above you. But what are you actually
looking at? And why is it so blue?

The atmosphere

Air blanket

When you see a blue sky, you're looking at
the Earth's atmosphere. It's the layer of air
that surrounds the whole planet, like a thick
blanket. Air contains a mixture of gases,
mainly oxygen and nitrogen. These gases are
made of tiny molecules. When bright sunlight
hits them, it makes them glow with blueish
light – and that's what you can see.

How big is the sky?

The atmosphere is thickest closest to the Earth. The higher
up you go, the thinner it gets, until there's hardly any air at all.
At about 100 kilometres high, the air is too thin for a plane to
fly, and much too thin to breathe. Most scientists agree that
space starts here. This boundary is called the Karman line. So
the main part of atmosphere is 100 kilometres high all around
the Earth. However, the sky also includes the Sun, Moon and
stars, so you could say it's as big as the whole of space.

Karman line

100 km

Upper layer of troposphere

11 km

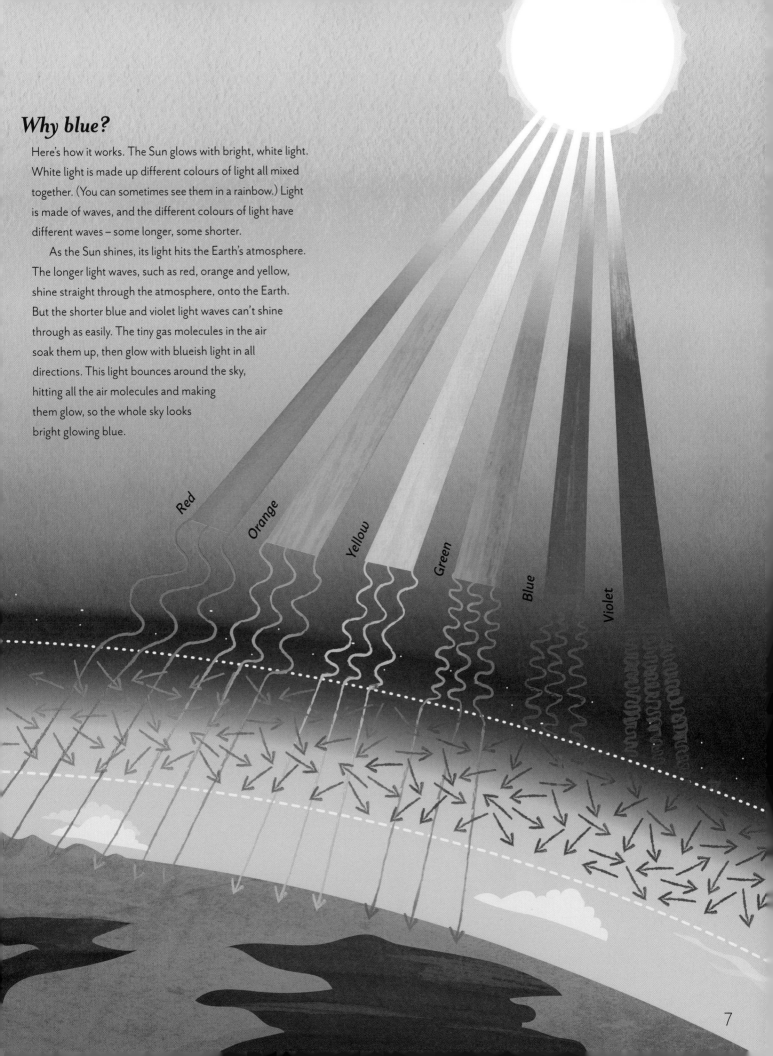

Why blue?

Here's how it works. The Sun glows with bright, white light. White light is made up different colours of light all mixed together. (You can sometimes see them in a rainbow.) Light is made of waves, and the different colours of light have different waves – some longer, some shorter.

As the Sun shines, its light hits the Earth's atmosphere. The longer light waves, such as red, orange and yellow, shine straight through the atmosphere, onto the Earth. But the shorter blue and violet light waves can't shine through as easily. The tiny gas molecules in the air soak them up, then glow with blueish light in all directions. This light bounces around the sky, hitting all the air molecules and making them glow, so the whole sky looks bright glowing blue.

Red

Orange

Yellow

Green

Blue

Violet

7

Ancient beliefs

Today we know a LOT about the sky, thanks to telescopes, weather balloons, satellites, and modern science. But long ago, people could only guess what the sky was made of, and how it worked.

Solid sky

Many ancient peoples believed that the sky was a solid dome, because that's how it looked! They thought the dome was like an upturned bowl, touching the round, flat Earth at the edges, and the Sun, Moon and stars could move around on the inside of that dome. These ideas were similar in several cultures around the world, even those that had never met each other.

The early ancient Greeks thought the dome was made of bronze, and in Finnish mythology, the blacksmith god Ilmarinen made it from steel. In the legends of Tahiti, the creator Taaroa emerged from a giant eggshell, and used that to make the sky dome.

Sky dome

Sun

The Sumerians and other cultures believed there were several layers of domes.

Stars

Moon

Earth

Many cultures thought the world was surrounded by endless oceans, including above the dome and below the land.

In some legends, such as those of the Navajo native Americans, windows in the dome could open to let in water from above, which became rain.

Windows

Some said the dome was supported on islands, or on a ring of high mountains around the edge of the world.

Underworld

The Earth was seen as flat, and usually round, forming the solid base of the dome.

Sky gods

Many ancient civilisations had a god of the sky. He or she was usually one of the most important of all gods, along with the Earth god, and lived in a heaven above the dome.

MAORI MYTHOLOGY: RANGI AND PAPA

Rangi is the Sky god, or Sky Father, in Maori legends. His wife is Papa, the Earth mother. At first, Rangi and Papa were close together, but their children, the gods of the sea, food and forests, pushed them apart into the positions they are in now. This allowed the daylight to shine between them.

ANCIENT EGYPT: NUT

The ancient Egyptian sky goddess Nut formed the sky with her own body. Her husband was Geb, the Earth god. Their children included the gods Osiris, Set and Isis.

MADAGASCAR: ZANAHARY

A story of the Malagasy people of Madagascar tells how the great sky god Zanahary worked with the Earth god, Ratovantany, to make humans. Ratovantany shaped their bodies from clay, and Zanahary gave them their souls. After people die, their bodies return to the Earth, and their souls return to the sky to live with Zanahary.

The Sun

The Sun is an enormous, burning hot ball of gas, constantly churning out light and heat. Without it, we wouldn't have day and night at all.

The Sun is HOT. In the middle, it's up to 15 million °C – 60,000 times hotter than a household oven. The surface is cooler, at 5,800 °C. But the corona, or outer atmosphere, is over 1 million °C.

What is the Sun?

The Sun is a star. It's like any other star, but much closer to us, so we see it as a giant, burning sphere. Like other stars, it's made of very hot gases, mostly hydrogen and helium. As hydrogen changes into helium, it releases vast amounts of energy in a constant, white-hot explosion.

Sunrise and sunset

Every morning, the Sun seems to "come up", as the Earth turns towards it. It's really just the Earth spinning, not the Sun movin But because you can't feel the Earth spinning, you see the Sun "rise", move across the sky, and then "set", or sink dow below the horizon in the evening.

Earth
Earth is the third-closest planet to the Sun

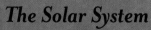

A year is the time it takes the Earth to orbit all the way around the Sun.

The Solar System

The Solar System means the Sun, and the planets and other objects that orbit around it. The Sun is in the middle. The way the Earth moves around the Sun gives us our days, nights and years.

As it orbits, the Earth spins. Each part of the world moves into the Sun's light, then out of it again, once every 24 hours.

This means that day and night are different in different parts of the world. When it's lunchtime in Peru, for example, it's midnight in Vietnam.

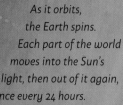

Day

Night

Core

Surface

Corona

THE SUN'S LIGHT IS SO BRIGHT THAT LOOKING STRAIGHT AT IT DAMAGES YOUR EYES.

150 million km

The Sun is about 150 million kilometres away from the Earth, on average. (It changes slightly, as we orbit around it in a slight oval). Although that's much closer than the other stars, it's still so far away that light coming from the Sun takes a whole eight minutes and 20 seconds to reach us.

The Sun is 1,390,000 kilometres across. It's so big that a million planet Earths could fit inside it.

Earth to scale
The size of the Earth.
compared to the Sun

Sun stories

The Sun was incredibly important to ancient people.
They had many stories about what it was.

ANCIENT EGYPTIAN

The Ancient Egyptians said that the sun god Ra sailed across the sky each day in a boat. At night, he sailed through the Underworld, where a giant serpent, Apep, tried to catch and eat him.

ABORIGINE

An Aboriginal story from northern Australia tells of Wuriupranili, the Sun Woman. Every morning she makes a campfire, then lights a torch from it and carries it across the sky.

INUIT

In Inuit legends, the Sun and Moon were a sister and brother, Malina and Anningan. They fell out, and Malina ran away and became the Sun in the sky. Anningan became the Moon and followed her. Every day and night, they chase each other across the sky.

Cloud spotting

Sometimes, the sky is a pure, empty blue. But more often, there are clouds to look at. They float fluffily along, blow across the sky in strong winds, or pile up ready for a storm. Clouds come in many different types, shapes and sizes, depending on how high up they are, the size of the water droplets, and the wind and other weather. You might spot all of these...

What are clouds?

Clouds are made of water. The Earth's atmosphere contains lots of water that has evaporated from oceans, lakes and rivers. It's also released from the leaves of plants and trees, and from animals, including humans, when we breathe out.

A lot of the water is in the form of a gas, called water vapour. But as water vapour gets higher and colder, it forms tiny liquid droplets, or ice crystals. They reflect and scatter all the white light from the Sun, and we see them as white clouds.

What about grey clouds?

Clouds can look grey or even black, especially when it's rainy or stormy. They aren't really grey, though – they are white like other clouds. Clouds that turn into rain, such as nimbostratus clouds, are usually quite low, thick, and full of large water droplets. This makes them seem grey, as not much sunlight can get through them from above. So they block out the sun, and their undersides are dark and shadowy.

Cumulonimbus
(meaning "heap of rain")
A giant cloud that reaches from low down to high up, bringing rain and sometimes thunder and lightning storms.

Stratus
(meaning "layer")
Low, flat, smooth clouds that "blanket" the sky

Nimbostratus
(meaning "rain layers")
Grey-looking, thick, flat rainclouds

Fog
A stratus-like cloud at ground level.

Cirrus
(meaning "hair-like")
High, thin, wispy clouds
made of ice crystals.

Cirrocumulus
(meaning "heap of hair")
High-up, little fluffy clouds
seen on sunny days

HIGH-LEVEL CLOUDS

CLOUD IN A JAR

A cloud forms when water vapour rises up into the sky, gets colder, and forms tiny droplets. You can make a mini cloud inside a jar in exactly the same way.

Strange and curious clouds

Sometimes, wind and weather conditions form clouds with bizarre and weird shapes These three strange clouds below are a rare sight...

Cirrostratus
(meaning "layers of hair")
Flat sheets of thin,
high-up cloud

6,000 metres
20,000 feet

YOU NEED:

A clear, clean glass jar with a lid
(such as an old jam jar)

Hot tap water

Ice cubes

A box of matches
(and an adult to help)

Mammatus
(meaning "udders")
Clouds covered in blobs that dangle down
underneath them, like giant water drops.

Altostratus
(meaning "high layers")
Large sheets of thin cloud

1. Put some hot tap water into the jar, about 3 cm deep.

2. Turn the lid of the jar upside-down, and put 3-4 ice cubes on it.

3. Ask an adult to strike a match, lower it into the jar, and drop it into the water.

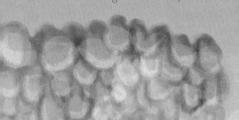

Altocumulus
(meaning "high heaps")
Patches or clumps of
mid-level cloud

4. Quickly put the upside-down lid and ice cubes on top of the jar.

5. Look through the side of the glass to see if you can see a cloud forming.

MID-LEVEL CLOUDS

Lenticular
(meaning "lentil-shaped")
Round clouds that can form over
mountaintops and are sometimes
mistaken for UFOs.

2,000 metres
6,500 feet

Stratocumulus
(meaning "layered heaps")
Large, low, cloudy clumps, and the
most common clouds on Earth

Volutus
(meaning "rolling")
A cloud shaped like a huge sausage or
rolling pin, most often spotted near coasts.

Cumulus
(meaning "heap")
Fluffy clouds like cotton wool,
seen in warm weather

LOW-LEVEL CLOUDS

The ice makes the water vapour get colder, and the match provides some tiny smoke particles that help the vapour condense into tiny droplets. If you take the lid off, the cloud may rise up into the air.

13

Water from the sky

We all need water. Humans, animals, plants and all other living things need it to survive. So it's pretty lucky, and miraculous, that the pure, clean water we need falls on us out of the sky! Some people hate rainy, cloudy days... But when water is scarce, everyone welcomes the rain.

How rain happens

Rain happens when the water droplets in clouds clump together, making bigger drops. When they're too heavy for the air to hold them up, they fall as raindrops.

Raindrops aren't actually shaped like this...

Actual size!

They are more like round, slightly squashed balls of water. The biggest raindrops can be one centimetre across.

Water recycling

Water from the sky goes around and around in the water cycle. Some soaks into the soil, and gets sucked up by the roots of plants and trees. Some runs into streams and rivers, and flows to the sea. Water evaporates from the sea, from the ground, and from plants' leaves, leaving behind sea salt, soil and dirt, in a natural cleaning process.

Precipitation

Weather scientists call water from the sky "precipitation". It's not just rain, but other kinds of precipitation too.

Snow
Water vapour that's got so cold high in the sky, it's frozen into fluffy ice crystals

Sleet
Partly frozen rain

Hail
Balls of solid ice, formed inside thunderclouds

Rainbows

Along with the rain comes the most amazing, beautiful sight in the sky... a rainbow! A rainbow forms when it's raining in one part of the sky... and sunny in another. If it stops raining, the rainbow vanishes. A rainbow is made when rays of sunlight hit the raindrops, and bounce around inside them. As the light rays change direction, they separate into bands of colour.

Rainbow tales

For as long as humans have told stories, we have tried to explain rainbows. In Australian Aboriginal mythology, the rainbow serpent curves through the sky as it moves from one waterhole to another. In old Hindu legends, the rainbow is a bow belonging to the thunder god Indra. He uses it to shoot bolts of lightning. In Japanese and Norse myths, rainbows were bridges linking the sky to the Earth.

MAKE A RAINBOW

You can use water to split sunlight into rainbow colours, and make your own mini rainbow patterns.

YOU NEED:
A glass of water

A small mirror, like a make-up mirror, that will fit into the glass (and that can get wet)

A piece of white paper

A window

A sunny day

1. Stand the glass of water on a sunny windowsill, or on a table where the sun can shine on it.

2. Put the piece of white paper next to the glass, on the same side as the window.

3. Put the mirror into the glass of water, facing the sun.

4. Tip and move the mirror around until it catches the sunlight and reflects it through the water. (Be careful not to reflect the sunlight into your eyes!)

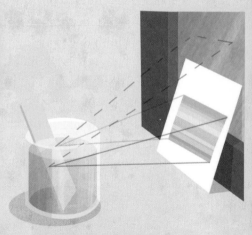

Where the sunlight shines onto the paper, you should see a mini rainbow of colours.

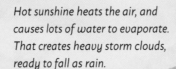

Hot sunshine heats the air, and causes lots of water to evaporate. That creates heavy storm clouds, ready to fall as rain.

Stormy skies

During a storm, the sky turns dark and fills with heavy rain, strong winds, and sometimes lightning and thunder too. A storm is a kind of extreme weather, usually with lots of rain and wind. Though storms usually count as bad weather, they start off thanks to sunshine and heat.

Thunder and lightning

A thunderstorm starts with a huge, piled-up cumulonimbus cloud. Ice crystals and hailstones move up and down inside the cloud. They rub together, building up an electric charge. Lightning is INCREDIBLY hot, up to 30,000°C. It heats up the air around it so much that it explodes outwards, making a super-loud sound wave. The booming noise seems to fill the whole sky. *Booooooooom!*

Don't get struck!

Lighting strikes the tallest point in an area, often tall buildings, trees and high-up places. Tall buildings have metal lightning conductors. They channel the electricity away from the building and down into the ground. So, in a thunderstorm, stay away from hilltops, trees and wide open spaces, and don't go up on the roof!

As the hot air rises, more air rushes in along the ground to replace it. This moving air makes wind.

Scary skies

Long ago, people used to think lightning happened because the gods were angry. For example, the Ancient Greeks believed the king of the gods, Zeus, used lightning as a weapon. Wherever lightning struck the ground was regarded as a sacred place.

Cyclones can be 500 km across. In the middle is the calm "eye of the storm".

Lightning is a giant electric spark that jumps between the cloud and the ground.

Monster storms

The biggest, deadliest storms are tropical cyclones – also called hurricanes or typhoons, depending on where in the world you are. A cyclone forms over warm ocean water, near the equator, where winds whip up giant waves. As the storm reaches land, it dumps vast amounts of water that floods the land. The roaring winds destroy trees and buildings.

Twister!

A tornado or twister is a funnel-shaped whirlwind. Tornadoes sometimes form below thunder clouds, when warm air spirals upwards. Tornadoes are usually quite small, but they can contain the fastest winds on the planet – sometimes over 500 km/h. The powerful wind can lift up people, animals, cars, and even bigger objects like train carriages or mobile homes!

Sometimes, during a thunderstorm or before a tornado, the sky can look dark green.

17

Strange skies

On the morning of 23 October 1947, in Marksville, Louisiana, USA, people were amazed to see fish raining down from the sky. But that's not the only odd occurrence, people all over the world have witnessed ghosts, falling frogs, strange substances and other peculiar things in our skies.

Eyewitness report

An animal scientist, Alexander Bajkov, was in the town at the time. He was having breakfast in a café when the fish rain began. He described how thousands of fish fell onto roads and rooftops, and even landed on people in the streets. He collected some of them to study, and found there were several different species.

Animal rain is rare, but maybe not as weird as it seems. It probably happens when some kind of tornado or other strong wind lifts up fish, frogs or other animals from the sea or a river, and carries them a short way, before they fall back down. But it's hard to be sure, as no one has seen that happening!

Animal rain

One case of animal rain is strange enough, but it's actually happened many times around the world. For example...

Fish fell on Sri Lanka 2014, and Lajamau, Australia, in 2010

There were showers of frogs in Serbia in 2005, and in Birmingham, England in 1892

Jellyfish fell on Bath, England in 1894

Tadpole rain fell in Japan in 2009

Even the Ancient Greeks and Romans reported fish and frog rain.

Spooky star jelly

Star jelly is an old name for mysterious white or grey jelly-like blobs that appear on the ground. According to folklore, star jelly falls from the sky the morning after showers of shooting stars have been spotted. Some say star jelly isn't actually from the sky – it's just a kind of slimy mould that can form on the grass. But blobs of jelly did fall from the sky onto Oakville, Washington, USA in 1994 – according to eyewitnesses. No one knows what they were!

Ships in the air

For centuries, sailors have described seeing ghostly ships sailing through the sky, far out to sea. Tales like these probably created legends such as the famous *Flying Dutchman*, a cursed ghost ship. These sightings are not made up – it really is possible to see a ghostly ship sailing in the sky. It's caused by a type of mirage, called a Fata Morgana.

You're actually seeing a real ship that's sailing beyond the horizon. Light rays from the ship get bent as they move between layers of warm and cold air above the sea surface. To people on this ship, it looks like a faint image of a ship is in the sky.

GHOST COIN

This simple experiment helps to show how a mirage works.

YOU NEED:
A medium-sized bowl that's not transparent
A coin
A bottle or jug of water

1. Put the coin in the bottom of the bowl.

2. Sit looking at the bowl so that you can see inside it, but can't see the bottom where the coin is.

3. Staying in the same position, pick up the water and put it into the bowl (or ask someone else to do this).

4. The coin will appear!

When the water is added to the bowl, it creates two layers – a layer of air and a layer of water. As the light rays from the coin pass through these layers, they bend towards you, and you can see the coin. Like a mirage, the bending light makes the coin appear to be in a different place from where it really is.

Birds of the air

The wing surface is mostly made of flat, light feathers.

Most birds have lightweight legs that are small or skinny.

For thousands of years, humans have watched birds flying in the sky, and wondered how they do it. If only we could fly like them! This amazing sight is a murmuration, a huge group of thousands of starlings. Each bird follows the movement of the birds around it, in a split second. The flock swoops, turns and changes shape, all moving as one.

Bird bodies

Birds have bodies built for flying. They have big, strong chest muscles to power their wings, and their bones are hollow, strong and light. If you compare the weight of a bird with a similar-sized mammal, the mammal will be around four times heavier!

Flying in flocks

Birds that migrate long distances often fly high in the sky in a giant V shape. You can often see ducks, geese and ibises doing this. But why? Flying in a V helps them to save energy. Each bird pushes the air just behind it downwards as it flies. But the air to the sides swirls upwards. By flying behind and to one side, the next bird can ride on the upwards-moving air. The birds take turns at the front, where it's hardest to fly.

How do birds fly?

Birds fly in two main ways: flapping and gliding. A bird that flaps its wings downwards spreads outs its wings and feathers, which pushes air down, and lifts the bird. As it flaps upwards, it folds its wings slightly, and angles its feathers so that air can slip through.

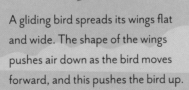

A gliding bird spreads its wings flat and wide. The shape of the wings pushes air down as the bird moves forward, and this pushes the bird up.

HIGHEST FLYER

Ruppell's vulture is the highest-flying bird on record. One was spotted flying 11,300 m up in the air (that's over 11 km high!).

HIGHEST MIGRATOR

Bar-headed geese fly over the Himalayas when they migrate, and reach heights of over 6,000 m.

LONGEST FLIGHT

The common swift lives mostly in the sky. It even sleeps while flying, and can stay in the air for as long as 10 months without landing.

WIDEST WINGSPAN

The wandering albatross glides over the sea on the longest wings in the bird world – up to 3.7 m across.

Insects and spiders

When you look up into the sky, you often see birds and aeroplanes. But you're also looking up at flying insects – millions and millions of them. They fly around to find food, mates, migrate or escape from danger. But because they're small, they can be hard to see!

Damselfly

Hoverfly

Fly like a fly

Not all insects have wings, but most do and are good at flying. That's why so many of them are called "flies"! Unlike birds, insects don't have feathers. Their super-lightweight wings are made from thin layers of chitin, a natural body substance a bit like plastic.

Cranefly

Monarch butterfly

Ladybird

Honeybee

A typical insect holds its body diagonally, with its head at the top. The wings flip back and up, then forward and down.

Swarm!

When insects fly in a big group, or swarm, it's easier to see them, as they fill the air. Honeybees swarm when their queen leaves the nest to look for a new home. Midges and mosquitoes lay their eggs in water, and when the adults emerge, they fly into the sky in huge clouds. Locusts form the biggest swarms – a swarm can be bigger than a city! As many as 10 billion locusts, which look like large grasshoppers, get together to search for food. The sky turns dark as the locusts descend to feed on farmers' crops.

Millions of monarch butterflies migrate together to their breeding areas, filling the air with orange wings.

What about spiders?

Spiders can't fly – can they? For people who don't like spiders, that's a scary idea! Spiders don't have wings, but they can fly through the sky by "ballooning". Young spiders, called spiderlings, do this to spread out and find new places to live.

FLY-GAZING

Ask an adult to catch a fly, daddy-long-legs or other insect in a clear glass, using a card to hold it inside. (It's better not to do this with stinging insects like bees and wasps!) Then you can use a magnifying glass to have a close look at the insect's amazingly fine, delicate wings. They are so thin, they're see-through.

Make sure to let the insect go free, when you're done investigating.

Red and white giant flying squirrel
Flying squirrels glide on stretched-out flaps of skin along the sides of their bodies, called "patagia". China's red and white giant flying squirrel has some of the biggest!

Paradise flying snake
This snake spreads its body out flat, like a wing, and "swims" through the air.

Graceful gliders

There are plenty of flying birds, bats and insects. But what if you looked up into the sky, and saw a lizard flying overhead? Or a snake, a frog or a squirrel?

Flying without wings

Some non-flying animals are able to glide. They can't take off from the ground and flap upwards. But if they are high up, they can glide safely downwards – for example to travel from one tree to another, or down to the ground. They do this using body parts that can spread out wide and flat, helping them to catch the air.

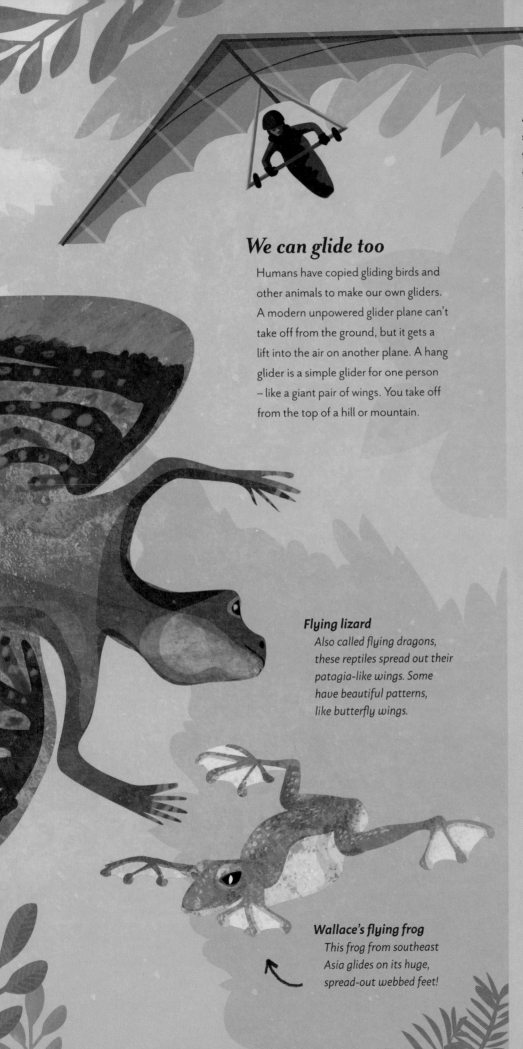

We can glide too

Humans have copied gliding birds and other animals to make our own gliders. A modern unpowered glider plane can't take off from the ground, but it gets a lift into the air on another plane. A hang glider is a simple glider for one person – like a giant pair of wings. You take off from the top of a hill or mountain.

Flying lizard
Also called flying dragons, these reptiles spread out their patagia-like wings. Some have beautiful patterns, like butterfly wings.

Wallace's flying frog
This frog from southeast Asia glides on its huge, spread-out webbed feet!

MAKE A KITE

A kite works like a glider too. The string holds it at the right angle, so that the wind can push against it and flow downwards, lifting the kite up.

YOU NEED:

Two thin, straight sticks, about 50 cm long and 40 cm long
A large sheet of paper, or an old plastic bag
Lots of strong, thin string
Sticky tape
Scissors

1. Tie the sticks together with string in the middle. Then tie string around the sticks to make a diamond-shaped frame.

2. Lie the frame on the paper or plastic, and cut around it, leaving an extra 3 cm around the edges. Fold the edges over the strings and tape them down.

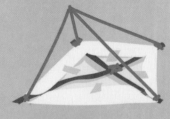

3. Tie two pieces of string loosely to the sticks like this, so that they meet in the middle. Finally, tie a much longer piece of string to the middle point.

4. Fly your kite!

Balloons and blimps

On 21 November, 1783, humans flew freely through the air for the first time, on board one of the first ever hot air balloons. Before this, the only human "flights" had been made by people jumping off towers wearing home-made wings. If they were lucky, they glided a little way, before crashing to the ground.

The two passengers, scientist Pilatre de Rozier and army officer Francois Laurent d'Arlandes, flew for 9 km and landed safely.

Into the air

In the 1780s, two French brothers, Joseph and Etienne Montgolfier, began experimenting with cloth and paper balloons filled with hot air. After a test flight carrying a sheep, a duck and a rooster went well, humans took to the skies. And you can still see hot air balloons in the sky to this day.

Modern hot air balloon

Cold air molecules

Hot air molecules

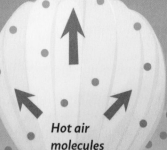

At the bottom of the balloon, burning fuel keeps the air hot.

Hot air

Hot air balloons work because as air heats up, its molecules spread out, making it lighter than cold air. A balloon filled with hot air floats upwards, just like a bubble of air in water.

Some balloons today have crazy shapes.

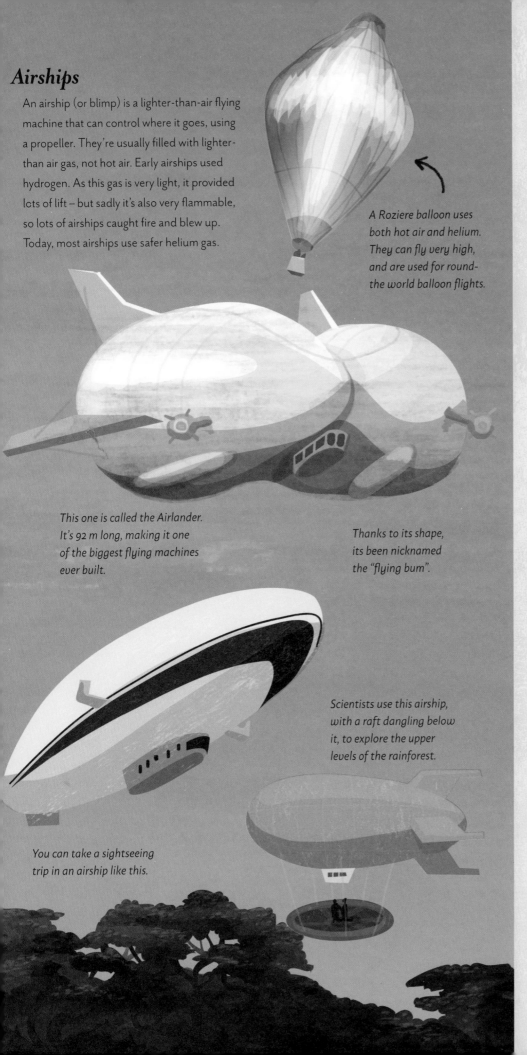

Airships

An airship (or blimp) is a lighter-than-air flying machine that can control where it goes, using a propeller. They're usually filled with lighter-than air gas, not hot air. Early airships used hydrogen. As this gas is very light, it provided lots of lift – but sadly it's also very flammable, so lots of airships caught fire and blew up. Today, most airships use safer helium gas.

A Roziere balloon uses both hot air and helium. They can fly very high, and are used for round-the world balloon flights.

This one is called the Airlander. It's 92 m long, making it one of the biggest flying machines ever built.

Thanks to its shape, its been nicknamed the "flying bum".

Scientists use this airship, with a raft dangling below it, to explore the upper levels of the rainforest.

You can take a sightseeing trip in an airship like this.

HEAT SPIRAL

Make this decorative spiral to show how hot air rises.

YOU NEED:

A large piece of thin card, A ruler, Pens, Scissors, String, A hot radiator

1. Use the ruler and a pen to draw a line of dots across the middle of the paper, 2 cm apart, like this.

2. Starting at the middle dot, draw a spiral, using the dots to help you draw it neatly.

3. Cut out the spiral and cut along the line all the way to the middle.

4. Ask an adult to make a small hole through the card in the middle of the spiral.

5. Cut a piece of string about 60 cm long and tie a knot in one end. Thread the other end through the hole so that you can hang the spiral up, like this.

Now ask an adult to hold or hang the spiral up above a warm radiator. As the warm air rises, it pushes against the sliding underneath of the spiral and makes it spin around. You can also do this experiment by holding the spiral above a candle flame.

Planes and helicopters

In 1783, it totally blew people's minds that anyone could fly through the sky. Today, most of us have done it, thanks to passenger planes, and have become used to flying round the world. But there is a problem – planes burn a lot of fuel, and release a lot of greenhouses gases, which adds to global warming. So, in the future, we'll probably have to fly a lot less.

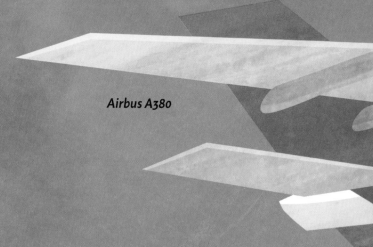

Airbus A380

First, pioneers such as George Cayley built simple gliders that could fly a short way from the top of a hill.

The first planes

Trying to make wings that flapped didn't help us to fly. The key to flying like a bird was to make fixed, spread-out wings, like those of a gliding bird. Once inventors realised this, planes took off!

American brothers Orville and Wilber Wright built and flew the first engine-powered plane in 1903. This led to fighter planes, cargo planes and passenger planes.

How does a plane fly?

Just like a gliding bird, a plane can fly thanks to the sharp and angle of its wings. As the plane zooms forward, the wings push air down, and this in turn pushes the plane up. This is why planes can only fly when they are going fast.

The plane is pushed up, against the force of gravity.

Air flowing over the top of the wing also flows downwards off the end of the wing.

Air hits the underside of the wing and gets forced downwards.

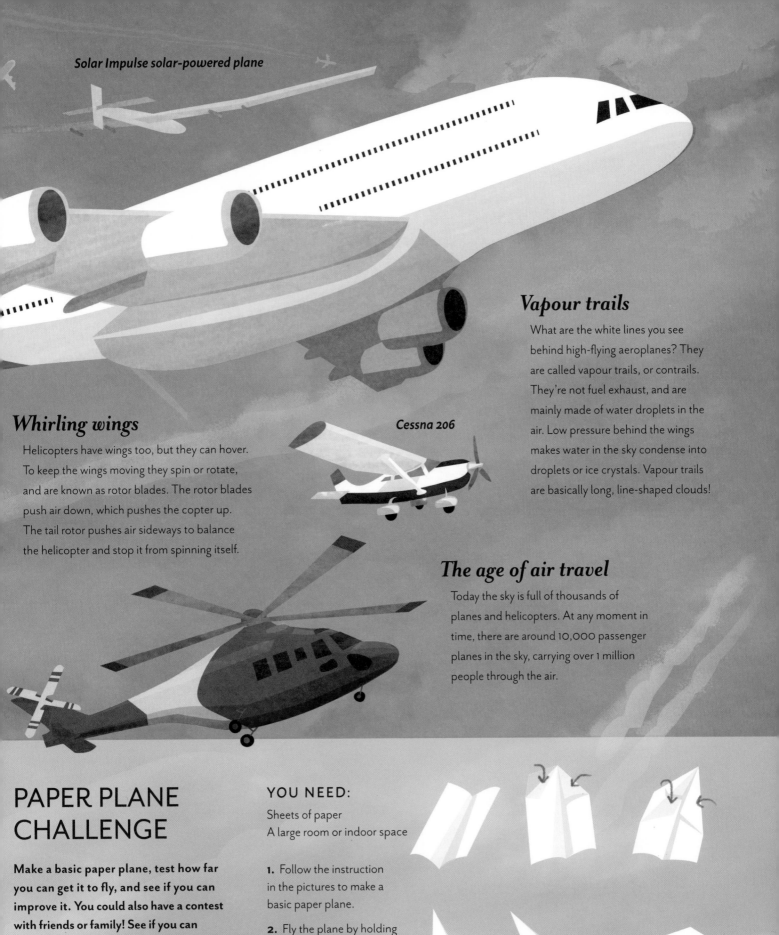

Solar Impulse solar-powered plane

Whirling wings

Helicopters have wings too, but they can hover. To keep the wings moving they spin or rotate, and are known as rotor blades. The rotor blades push air down, which pushes the copter up. The tail rotor pushes air sideways to balance the helicopter and stop it from spinning itself.

Cessna 206

Vapour trails

What are the white lines you see behind high-flying aeroplanes? They are called vapour trails, or contrails. They're not fuel exhaust, and are mainly made of water droplets in the air. Low pressure behind the wings makes water in the sky condense into droplets or ice crystals. Vapour trails are basically long, line-shaped clouds!

The age of air travel

Today the sky is full of thousands of planes and helicopters. At any moment in time, there are around 10,000 passenger planes in the sky, carrying over 1 million people through the air.

PAPER PLANE CHALLENGE

Make a basic paper plane, test how far you can get it to fly, and see if you can improve it. You could also have a contest with friends or family! See if you can change your plane to make it fly further – try making flaps at the back, folding up the wingtips, or taping parts together.

YOU NEED:

Sheets of paper
A large room or indoor space

1. Follow the instruction in the pictures to make a basic paper plane.

2. Fly the plane by holding it up high and launching it forward. How far can you get it to go?

Hi-tech sky

Imagine having your own hi-tech flying machine! What if everyone had one, and we could all zoom around in the sky whenever we liked? It could be possible in the future – and you can already see some machines like this flying around.

The jet wingpack launches from a helicopter, and lands using a parachute.

Jetpacks

A jetpack is a jet engine that you wear on your back, allowing you to zoom straight up into the air. You can't fly for long though, as you can't carry very much fuel, and the engine makes you very heavy.

So far, jetpacks are only used for stunts and special displays.

The Flyboard Air
It's similar to a jetpack, but the rider stands on top of it.

Fuel is carried in a backpack

Hoverboards

In August 2019, French inventor Franky Zapata flew across the English channel, from France to England, on a hoverboard he had built, the Flyboard Air. It can fly up to 3,000 m high and reach a speed of over 150 km/h.

Human planes

Another inventor, Swiss pilot Yves Rossy, is famous for flying with a pair of jet-powered wings fixed to his back, called a jet wingpack. By moving his body, he can steer and fly up and down, and even loop the loop!

Drones

A drone is a small aircraft that flies by itself, with no crew. Drones can be piloted remotely by a human controller, or they can be robotic, and programmed to find their own way. Drones are incredibly useful, and they're a becoming more and more common sight in the sky. They can be used for mapping, search and rescue, aerial photography, deliveries, and for racing as a sport.

This design has several small rotors, like a large drone with a cockpit in the middle.

Flying car future

For decades, we've dreamed of flying cars that can carry us through the air and land anywhere. They feature in countless sci-fi movies as the transport of the future. Aircraft engineers have actually invented several types of flying cars. They have been tested and can fly – and some of them are even available to buy. So far though, flying cars are too expensive, and too hard to fly, for most normal people to have one.

Anti-gravity?

All flying machines have to push against gravity somehow, to lift up into the air and stay there. But if there was a device that could somehow reverse or switch off gravity, it would make flying much easier. Scientists are still trying to get to the bottom of how gravity really works... but one day, "anti-gravity" machines could exist.

Dusk

As the part of the Earth where you live turns away from the Sun, the daytime ends, and the sky gets dark. From your position on Earth, you see the Sun appear to sink below the horizon, or set.

Fiery sunsets

As the Sun sets, the sky around it often looks orange or pink. This is because the Sun is at a low angle, and its light has to travel through more of the atmosphere to reach you. The air molecules in the atmosphere scatter all the purple, blue and green light so much, only the red, yellow, and orange light can get through.

Up with the dawn

As dawn breaks, the daylight wakes up diurnal animals – those that are active during the day. Birds and insects begin flying out to look for food, and male songbirds start singing, to attract a mate or to warn other males off their territory. In the countryside, cockerels really do wake everyone up by crowing at dawn. The loud singing of many different types of birds is called the dawn chorus.

First light

When the Sun finally begins to rise, the sky often looks pink. This is why the ancient Greek poet Homer often described dawn as having rosy fingers, or spreading pink blossoms across the sky. Like sunset, sunrise makes the sky pink because the Sun is at a low angle. As it shines through the atmosphere, the blue light is scattered away, and the pink and orange light reaches our eyes.

The gloaming

The time between day and night is known as dusk, twilight or the gloaming. As the sky darkens, the brightest stars and planets start to appear.

Crepuscular creatures

Animals that are active at dusk are known as "crepuscular". Bats, insects, and crepuscular birds flutter through the shadows as night falls.

The darkness before dawn

According to an old proverb, "the darkest hour is just before the dawn." This might be because sometimes, the Moon goes down before dawn, leaving a dark time before the Sun comes up. It could also be because some ancient peoples saw the time before dawn as scary and dangerous. In Anglo-Saxon times, the word *úhtcearu* meant "anxiety before dawn". In Swedish, the word *vargtimmen* is similar, and means "the time of the wolf".

Dawn

At last, the night comes to an end, as your part of the Earth moves back around into the Sun's light. Wherever you are in the world, as dawn breaks, the Sun appears to rise above the horizon in the east.

SKYGAZING

Illustrated by
KERRY HYNDMAN

Written by
ANNA CLAYBOURNE

For Berwyn, my little nature loving pal.
Kerry Hyndman

———

For Albireo and Io.
Anna Claybourne

CONTENTS

Night falls

As night falls, it cloaks everything in darkness. The dark can bring fear and mystery, as shadows hide and disguise the daytime world. Turning away from the Sun, we face the black vastness of space.

But not everything is dark. Houses and cities glow. The stars and planets shine and sparkle. The Moon seems so close, you could reach out and touch it. As daylight fades away, flying animals take to the skies, at ease in the dark. Bats and moths flutter in and out of the shadows, and owls glide and swoop on their nightly hunting trips. When you look at the night sky, you see into the most distant reaches of space, further away than we could ever travel. The sky is a map of the universe, and standing on the world, you are a part of it.

Dark skies

Night happens because the Earth spins around, once every 24 hours. As your part of the world turns away from the Sun, the sky grows dark. Of course, this means that not everyone has night at the same time.

Changing nights

Most parts of the world have seasons, with longer, darker nights in winter, and shorter nights in summer. This happens because the Earth is slightly tilted to one side. When your part of the Earth is tilted towards the Sun, it's summer. As the Earth spins round, making day and night, it gets more sunshine, and daylight lasts longer. The opposite happens in winter. Your part of the Earth is leaning away from the Sun. As the Earth spins, it only comes into the light for a short time.

N

N

Earth's orbit

South Pole

Equator

Sun

North Pole

The Earth orbits around the Sun,

and one full orbit makes a year.

On the equator

However, it's a bit different if you're near or on the equator, like the cities of Quito in Ecuador, or Mombasa in Kenya. As the Earth orbits the Sun, your position changes slightly, but you get a similar amount of daylight all year. In Quito, on the equator, the Sun always sets between 6 and 6.30pm all year round, and the night is always around 12 hours long.

Darkness all day

The further north or south you go, the longer the nights are in winter, and the shorter they are in summer. In fact, at the North and South Poles, winter is just one long night. For six months, there's no daylight at all.

SKYGAZING

To get a good look at the night sky, it's easiest if you lie down. You can do this on a clear, dry night, in a garden, a park or somewhere in the countryside, such as a campsite. (Make sure you have an adult with you!) Lie on the ground on a picnic mat or a large coat. Wait several minutes for your eyes to adjust to the darkness. What can you see?

Night stories

If you're scared of the dark, or find the night spooky, you're not alone. Humans have felt this way for the whole of our history. That's because the night IS scary. For prehistoric people, the darkness meant they couldn't find their way, or see dangers such as fierce wild animals. The Moon and stars must have seemed like magical lanterns, but no one knew what they really were.

Who put the stars there?

Many traditions tell how ancient gods, or the first people, put the stars in the sky.

THE GIRL AND THE ASHES

According to a San legend from southern Africa, long ago the night sky was completely dark. A girl, one of the early people, wanted more light, so that she could find her way at night. She took a handful of glowing embers from the fire, and threw them up into the sky, making the stars.

COYOTE AND THE STARS

An old Navajo story tells how First Man and First Woman began to arrange the stars carefully in the sky, making beautiful, bright patterns. But Coyote grew bored of waiting. He took the rest of the stars and threw them up into the sky all at once, so that they went everywhere. That's why some of the stars form constellations, but the rest are randomly scattered.

ORION AND THE SCORPION

In ancient Greek myths, the gods often put heroes and animals into the sky to become stars. For example, Orion, a great hunter, died when he was stung by a giant scorpion. Zeus made them both into constellations, which are now known as Orion and Scorpius.

The witching hour

When people believed in witches, many thought that they flew around and cast spells at night. The "witching hour" was between 3 and 4 o'clock in the morning. This is why witches are said to have night-loving animals, such as cats and bats, as their "familiars" or pets.

The day and the night

For many ancient peoples, the Sun and the daytime were male, while the Moon and night were female. In Norse mythology, the night is a giant named Nott. She is the mother of Dagr, the day, and she and her son take turns to ride across the sky. Nott's horse, Hrimfaxi, drips foam from his bit, which becomes the morning dew.

A legend from the Philippines tells how when Apolaki, the Sun, and Mayari, the Moon fought over who would rule the world, Mayari lost one of her eyes. Apolaki was filled with remorse, and from then on, he agreed to share the world with Mayari, ruling it by day while she ruled by night. But because she only has one eye, Mayari's light, the light of the Moon, is fainter.

Orion – the Hunter

Ursa Major – the Great Bear

Gemini – the Twins

Leo – the Lion

Starry sky

On a dark, clear night, when you look up at the sky, you're looking into an enormous universe of stars. Stars are burning, glowing balls of hot gas. They are so far away that they look like tiny, shining dots. But close-up, a typical star is BIG – over one million kilometres from side to side.

Star patterns

Constellations are the patterns we see in the stars. The stars in a constellation are not close together in space, but viewed from Earth, they seem to form a pattern or shape. You can see different constellations from different parts of the Earth. Each star and constellation has its own name, which often comes from old Arabic or Latin words.

The Milky Way

In space, stars form huge clusters called galaxies. The stars we can see in the night sky belong to our own galaxy, a giant, whirling, flattened disk of stars called the Milky Way. It gets its name because on a very clear night, you can see a thick band of stars, like a white path across the sky. This is the view towards the middle of the Milky Way, where the most stars are.

Lupus – the Wolf

Southern Cross

Scorpius – the Scorpion

The Teapot

This is Antares, one of the stars in the constellation Scorpius. It's an old star, in the Red Supergiant stage of its life, giving it a reddish glow.

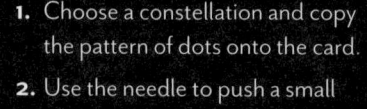

Sagittarius – the Archer

CONSTELLATION CARDS

Create your own constellations on your bedroom wall!

YOU NEED:

Postcard-sized pieces of card

A pen or pencil

A needle

A torch

1. Choose a constellation and copy the pattern of dots onto the card.

2. Use the needle to push a small hole through each dot.

3. In a dark room, shine the torch at the card to make the constellation appear on the wall.

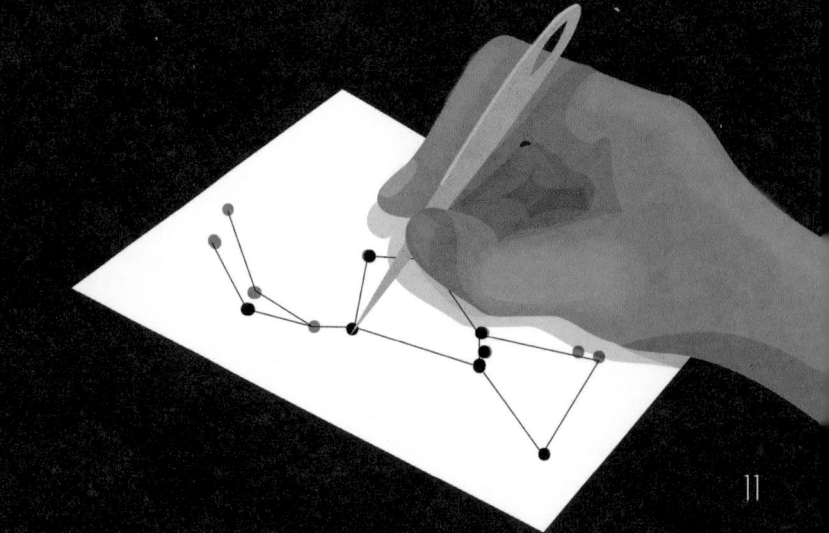

11

The planets orbit the Sun at different speeds and distances. As they move around, they appear in different positions when viewed from Earth.

Uranus

Orbit path

Jupiter is mostly made of hydrogen and helium gas.

Jupiter

Mercury

Venus

Sun

Neptune

The planets

Long ago, when people stared up at the night sky, they noticed that while most stars stayed in fixed positions, a few moved around. They became known as the planets, meaning "wanderers". Of course, as we know now, the planets are not stars at all.

Planets in the sky

In the night sky, planets do look bright and twinkly, like the stars, even though they don't glow. This is because they reflect the light from the Sun. You can't always see all the planets, because of the way they move around – but you can often see some of them. Venus looks like a very big, bright star – brighter than any other object in the sky, apart from the Sun and Moon.

Mars is made of rock, iron and ice.

Mars

Earth

Saturn

What are planets?

Planets are large, round space objects, or worlds, like the Earth. Unlike stars, they do not burn, glow and give off energy. They are mostly made of rock, water, gas or ice, or a mixture of those things. The planets we can see are part of the Solar System, and orbit around our star, the Sun. That's why they seem to "wander" and move across the sky.

SPOTTING PLANETS

To look at planets in the night sky, you need to find out which ones are visible, and where they are. Astronomy and space websites post updates on where to look for them. You can also get apps that help you find planets and stars.

Binoculars will give you a better view. To use them, first find the planet you want to look at without using the binoculars, then try to line up or "train" the binoculars on it. It helps to lie down in the ground, or lean on something like a fence or windowsill to keep the binoculars steady.

With a good pair of binoculars, you could see:

VENUS
looking like the Moon, as it reflects the sun on one side.

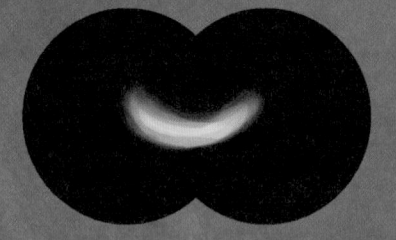

JUPITER
and its four closest moons, which look like dots of light.

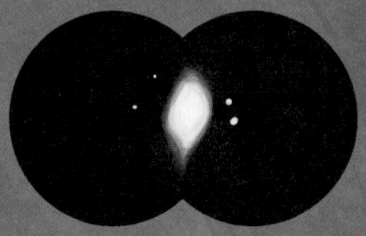

SATURN
The wide shape of Saturn and its rings.

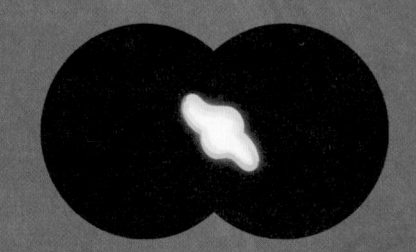

The Moon orbits the Earth roughly once every 28 days.

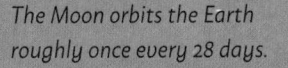

The Moon

The Moon is the biggest, brightest object you can see in the night sky. Like the planets, it reflects the Sun's light, and seems to shine.

Moon movements

The Moon is like a mini-planet. It orbits the Earth, just as the Earth orbits the Sun. At the same time, as the Earth spins around, we see the Moon rise and set every 24 hours. All this means that the Moon is always appearing in different places in the sky, sometimes in the day, and sometimes at night. However, we're more likely to notice it at night, as when the rest of the sky is dark, the Moon looks brighter.

Who's in the Moon?

The Moon has patterns on it, made up of craters and flat areas. Some people see a "Man in the Moon", while in some cultures, they say it's a rabbit. What can you see?

Faraway Moon

In diagrams, the Moon is shown close to the Earth, but it's actually a very long way away. The Moon is about 3,474 kilometres across – a quarter of the size of the Earth, and it's about 385,000 kilometres away.

Moon

Earth

385,000 km

Waxing quarter
or Half Moon

Waxing gibbous
(meaning a growing swollen Moon)

Waxing crescent
(meaning a growing crescent Moon)

Phases of the Moon

As the Moon travels around the Earth, we see different amounts of it lit up by the Sun, and its appearance changes. These changes are called the phases of the Moon.

Full Moon

New Moon

You can't see a New Moon, as it's in the same direction as the Sun and we can't see any reflected light. The full Moon appears when the Moon is opposite the Sun, so we see it at night.

Waning gibbous
(meaning a shrinking swollen Moon)

Waning quarter
or Half Moon

Waning crescent
(meaning a shrinking crescent Moon)

MODEL THE MOON

This activity makes it easy to see why the Moon changes shape.

YOU NEED:

A lamp

A white ball, such as a ping pong ball

A dark room

Stand in the dark room, next to the lamp. The lamp represents the Sun, and you are the Earth.

Hold up the ball so that it's in line between your eyes and the lamp.

Now slowly turn around, looking at the ball.

You'll see the ball lit up on one side when it's near the lamp, like a crescent Moon – changing to a fully lit up "full Moon" when you're facing away from the lamp.

Strange sights

What does it mean if you see a falling star, strange lights moving in a pattern, or a night rainbow?

Shooting stars

A falling star, or shooting star, looks like a star zooming across the sky. But it's not a star! It's a meteor – a small lump of dust or rock falling into the Earth's atmosphere. As a meteor falls, it hits air molecules and heats up, burning white hot until it's all gone.

Neptune's orbit

Orbit of Halley's comet

Sun

Earth's orbit

Old beliefs

It's traditional to make a wish when you see a shooting star. But when people long ago saw comets, they usually thought it meant a disaster was on the way. In 1066, King Harold of England died in the Battle of Hastings – not long after Halley's comet appeared. It was seen as a warning of his doom, and was depicted flying over Harold's head in the Bayeux tapestry.

Comets

A comet is a ball of dust and ice that orbits the Sun. When it's near the Sun, we can see it in the sky. The Sun makes some of the ice evaporate, forming the comet's "tail". Unlike a meteor, a comet doesn't appear to move fast. This is because, like the planets, it's much farther away than a meteor. Halley's Comet appears once every 75 or 76 years. It was here in 1986, and will return in 2061. Maybe you can look out for it!

Moon marvels

A Blood Moon happens during a lunar eclipse, when the Earth blocks out the Sun and casts a shadow on the Moon. Some sunlight still shines around the Earth, but the atmosphere scatters the blue and green light. Only reddish light reaches the Moon, making it look red.

A rare Moonbow is a rainbow created by moonlight, instead of sunlight. It happens when a bright full Moon shines onto raindrops or waterfall spray.

In 1989 and 1990, people in Belgium reported seeing triangle-shaped pattern of lights in the sky.

Strange lights often appear above Hessdalen, a valley in Norway. No one is sure what they are.

UFOs

If something strange appears in the sky and no-one knows what it is, it's a UFO! UFO stands for Unidentified Flying Object. Though some people put UFOs down to alien spaceships visiting Earth, there are lots of other possible explanations, such as aircraft lights, satellites, lightning, birds, balloons, and even clouds.

SEE A METEOR SHOWER

As the Earth orbits the Sun, it passes through clouds of dust left by comets. This creates "meteor showers" of many shooting stars. If you want to see one, check space websites such as **space.com** and **nasa.gov** to find when they happen in your part of the world. The Perseids meteor shower is visible in the Northern hemisphere around 12th August. The Geminids can be seen from both hemispheres around 14th December.

Bats take flight

Around the world, as the Sun goes down,
billions and billions of bats wake up,
and fly out into the night sky to feed.

Bat hunting

These bats are heading out to feed
on night-flying insects, like moths
and mosquitoes. This helps farmers,
if they have crops that moths feed
on. It also reduces the number of
mosquitoes that bite people and
animals and spread diseases.

Bats have an unusual way of
finding food in the dark, called
echolocation. They make high-
pitched squeaks, then listen for the
echoes as the sound bounces off
objects. Using echolocation, a bat
can find, chase and catch a moth
with deadly accuracy.

Bat's squeak

*Echo reflected
from moth*

How bats fly

Bats don't have feathery wings like birds. Instead,
their wings are made of thin, leathery skin stretched
over their arm and hand bones. The bat's thumb
claw is used as a hook to help it climb and hang
upside down.

Bat cave

Not all bats live in caves, but they are often home to huge bat groups, or colonies. One of the most famous is Bracken Cave in Texas, USA, where over 20 million Mexican free-tailed bats roost, or sleep, during the day. The bats pour out of their cave in the evening. When a colony of bats leave their roost to feed, it's called a "bat exodus". Some bats roost in other places, like abandoned buildings, churches, or under bridges.

Giant fruit bats

Bats are not all hunters. Some are vegetarians, like giant fruit bats, also known as flying foxes. They roost in trees during the day, and fly out at night to look for fruit, flowers and nectar. In Indonesia or the Philippines, you could see a flying fox with a wingspan of up to 1.5 metres soaring overhead.

Blind as a bat

Though people sometimes use the phrase "blind as a bat", bats are not blind! Some have quite good eyesight – they just have brilliant hearing as well.

HUMAN ECHOLOCATION

Humans can learn to use echolocation too, though we are not as good at it as bats.

YOU NEED:

A cardboard tube

A metal mixing bowl or baking tray

A blindfold

Someone to test you

1. Ask your helper to blindfold you.
2. Hold up the tube and sing or shout into it.
3. Your helper should move the bowl or tray in front of the other end of the tube, then away again, while you keep making a noise.
4. Can you tell when it's there, from the change in sound? You are detecting the echo, just like a bat.

Barn Owl
This common owl is one of the easiest to see at night, thanks to its pale feathers.

Owls have large eyes, but to hunt, they mainly use their ears, which are hidden deep under their feathers.

Fringe-like feathers along the back edges of an owl's wings soak up and muffle the sounds of its wingbeats.

Birds of the night

While most bats are nocturnal, or active at night, most birds are not. Only a few come out to find food in the dark – and most of these are owls.

The dish shape of an owl's face reflects sounds into its ears.

Silent flight

Owls are large birds of prey. They hunt at night, listening for small animals such as voles and field mice, and swooping down to grab them. Barn owls are found almost everywhere in the world. To help it sneak up on prey, a barn owl can fly almost completely silently. It can hear a mouse as it scurries along the ground when it's flying 30 metres above them.

Potoo
In the rainforests of South and Central America, the strange-looking Potoo rests during the day, disguised as part of a tree branch, with its huge eyes closed. At night it takes flight and snaps up insects.

Bat hawk

Night flyers

Besides owls, there are some other birds that fly by night. The bat hawk has evolved to feed on bats in flight. Though its beak is small, it has a huge mouth so that it can swallow a bat whole while still in the air!

Migrating by moonlight

Some day-flying birds, such as thrushes, buntings and geese do sometimes fly at night – when they are migrating long distance. At night it's cooler, and there are fewer hungry birds of prey around (apart from owls and bat hawks). Scientists think some birds can also use the stars to help them find their way, as sailors used to do at sea. Astronomers looking at the Moon sometimes see high-flying migrating birds flying in front of it, like these snow geese.

Nighthawk

Like bats, nighthawks set out at dusk to fly high in the sky, chasing and catching insects. They hunt using their eyesight, and to make this easier, they sometimes feed on fireflies.

LISTEN FOR OWLS

It can be hard to spot owls at night, but you're much more likely to hear them. If you have trees, parks or woodland near your home, you can listen from a window or garden. You can often hear owls when you're camping, too. In most parts of the world, you could hear one or more of these:

BARN OWL
Skreeeecchhh!
A loud, rattling shriek

SHORT-EARED OWL
Wowk! Yerp! Hoo-hoo-hoo
Short yelps and hoots

LONG-EARED OWL
Eeeeeoooo
A long, high-pitched squeak

GREAT HORNED OWL
Hu-hoo, hoo, hoo
Series of low hoots

EAGLE OWL
Hoo-hoouuuu. Wa-wa-wa
Long, low hoots and quacks

SNOWY OWL
Wow - wow - wak wak wak
Similar to a dog bark and a duck quack!

GREAT GREY OWL
Hu - hu - hu
A short, low hoot, like a train whistle

LITTLE OWL
Hoooo... hoooo.. eep eep
A flute-like echoing call

TAWNY OWL
Twit-twooooo!
Classic owl "hoot"

Night-flying bugs

At night, many insects seem to disappear. Butterflies, wasps, bees and dragonflies go home to their nests, or rest on plants or trees. Then, as it gets dark, you'll see and hear other insects flying through the night.

Sensitive feathery antennae detect the scent of the food and help them find a mate.

Polyphemus moth

Why fly at night?

Some insects, like most moths, have evolved to fly at night because it has advantages for them. It's harder for predators to find and eat them, and there are fewer other bugs around to compete for food.

But there are some disadvantages, too. At night it's colder, darker and harder to see. So nocturnal moths have adapted to survive.

Many moths have grey and brown patterns to give them camouflage... but not all. Here are some of the amazing moths you could see flying by.

The scales on moths' wings are bigger and act like fur, helping to keep in warmth.

Fluffy wings may also make it harder for bats to detect them with echolocation.

Giant Leopard moth
The beautiful, black and white-spotted giant leopard moth of North and Central America.

Atlas moth
The Atlas moth from South and Southeast Asia, the biggest in the world.

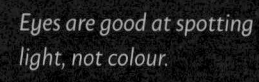
Eyes are good at spotting light, not colour.

Elephant Hawk moth
The velvety pink and gold elephant hawk moth, found in Europe and Asia.

Luna moth
The Luna moth, a lime green North American moth with long "tails" on its wings.

Why do moths love lights?

At night, moths often fly towards lights and candle flames. This could be because moths navigate by the Moon and stars, and our bright lights confuse them. Or maybe bright lights remind moths of white flowers where they can feed on nectar. No one knows for sure.

Night biters

Some mosquitoes and midges fly at night, too. They are delicate insects that like to be near water, as the heat of the day can make them dry out. The use their sense of smell in the dark to home in on sleeping animals or people to bite and feed on.

Glowing at night

Fireflies are a type of beetle. They can flash light from their tails to signal to each other when they are looking for a mate. At night in the parks, gardens and meadows where fireflies live, they fill the air with flashing, glowing dots.

Firefly

GO MOTHING

In summer, try "mothing" – attracting moths with a white sheet, so you can look at them closely. You need a garden, campsite, or other safe outdoor space.

Hang an old white sheet up on a washing line, or between two trees or bushes, or just drape it over a chair. Shine a bright torch light at the sheet to light it up. After a while, moths will be drawn to the light and will come and rest on the sheet.

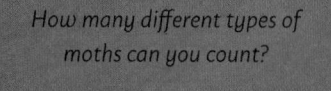

How many different types of moths can you count?

Try drawing them or taking photos.

Into space

Long ago, humans couldn't fly at all. Then we invented balloons, planes and helicopters to fly in the air. Finally, less than 100 years ago, we began to go into space, using rockets. A rocket launch can happen during the day or night, but at night it's easier to see the path of the rocket from its trail of burning fuel.

The delivery module is now in orbit

The first stage falls back to the ground to be re-used

The second stage separates here

Falcon rocket

How rockets work

The main part of a space rocket is a long tube full of fuel. As the fuel burns, it pushes gases downwards, and they push the rocket up. As the fuel gets used up, the fuel tanks drop away in stages.

Journeys to space

Since the first rocket launches, we've sent space missions further and further away from the Earth. But we've still only managed to explore a tiny part of the sky. Space is so huge that is would take millions of years, using today's technology, to reach the faraway stars and galaxies.

1961
The first astronaut, Yuri Gagarin, enters orbit

1966
A Venus space probe is the first object to land on another planet

1969
Neil Armstrong and Buzz Aldrin walk on the Moon

The darkness of space

Whether you launch by day or by night, once you reach space, about 100 kilometres above the Earth's surface, the sky is dark. The daytime sky we see from Earth looks blue because of sunlight shining through the Earth's atmosphere. But in outer space, and on the Moon, there's no atmosphere. The Sun is still there, but it's surrounded by blackness.

This SpaceX Falcon 9 rocket *launched at night in March 2020, carrying supplies to the International Space Station.*

POP ROCKET

This rocket works like a real one, using a chemical reaction to make the gas.

YOU NEED:

A tube-shaped plastic container with a pop-off top

A fizzing vitamin tablet or a chunk of bath bomb

An outdoor space

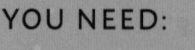

1. Take the lid off the container and half-fill it with water.
2. Quickly drop the tablet or bath bomb in, press the lid on, and stand it upside down on the ground. (Ask an adult to do this bit if you like)
3. Stand back!

The tablet or bath bomb fizzes and releases bubbles of gas in the water. The gas builds up and pushes the lid downwards, making the container shoot upwards.

Sputnik 1 was the first human-made satellite. It was launched into orbit in 1957.

Sky full of satellites

A satellite is an object that orbits around another object in space. For example, the Moon is a natural satellite of the Earth. Now, though, there are also thousands of artificial satellites in the sky. Over 5,000 satellites are constantly criss-crossing the sky over our heads.

What do satellites do?

Satellites in orbit can do all kinds of things that are more difficult to do from the ground. Weather forecasting, smartphones, the Internet, TV streaming and car satnavs all work using satellites, and scientists use them to study both Earth and space.

AURA

Earth observation satellites take pictures of the Earth and measure things such as cloud patterns, snow cover and temperature. Aura checks the ozone layer and air quality, keeping track of climate change.

MEXSAT Bicentenario

Communications satellites such as this one transmit messages and signals around the world.

Our home in space

The biggest, most complex satellite of all is the International Space Station, where astronauts can live and work in space. It's made up of units which have been added over time, each on a separate rocket flight. On board the ISS, astronauts live in microgravity (very low gravity) so they float around, and so do their tools, science equipment, food and possessions.

Hubble space telescope

Space telescopes such as Hubble and the James Webb telescope are put into orbit to get a better view of space.

Living and sleeping compartment

Solar panels

Canadarm 2 robot arm

Science labs

Framework

GPS Block III satellite

GPS (Global positioning system) satellites link to satnav or GPS receivers on the ground, showing exactly where they are.

ISS FLYBY

You can often see satellites in the sky at night, reflecting the Sun's light in the same way the Moon does. The ISS appears as a shining spot of light, like a bright star, moving across the sky. It circles the Earth roughly once every 90 minutes, and covers a slightly different path around the Earth each time. This means that you can see it from most parts of the world, if you look up at the right time!

To spot the ISS, check NASA's "Spot the Station" website at **spotthestation.nasa.gov**

Enter your home town, and the site will tell you if the ISS is passing overhead soon, and when and where to look for it.

City lights

When astronauts on the International Space Station look down at the Earth at night, they see all the cities light up by billions of electric lights.

Light pollution

Long ago, before we had electric lighting, people used candles and gas lamps, which didn't make so much light. Now, the night sky is often filled with lights, especially in cities and towns. This extra light is sometimes called light pollution. It's bad news for astronomers and stargazers, because it makes it harder to see the stars and other space objects. It's much easier to see them in truly dark places, like the middle of a desert.

Tall towers

Most large cities have tall skyscrapers and towers. These tall buildings have to display bright lights at night, to alert aircraft to where they are. They are also used for flashing light shows and firework displays.

The tail has a white light

The right wing has a green light and a white light

The left wing (from the captain's viewpoint) always has a red light and a white light

Boeing 737-900

Flying lights

The skies are also full of planes and helicopters, with their own bright lights. Aircraft have lights to make them visible to each other at night. If you're looking up at the night sky and you see a green light, a red light and white flashing lights, it's probably a passenger plane (although spacecraft have these lights too).

Too bright for nature

Bright lights at night can cause other problems too. They make it harder for humans to sleep deeply, which can be bad for our health. And they can confuse migrating animals. Birds sometimes crash into tall towers at night, perhaps mistaking their bright lights for starlight.

EYE-OPENER

This experiment shows how your eyes react to light and darkness.

YOU NEED:

A mirror in a dimly lit room
A bright lamp or torch

In dim light, face the mirror, and look at your pupils. After a while, switch on the torch and shine it at the mirror. Watch your pupils – what happens? Your pupils get wider in the dark, to let in more light.

Dim light   **Brighter light**

Pupil

Amazing auroras

There are all kinds of lights to see in the night sky... but most amazing and magical of all are the auroras. They are huge swirls and waves of light across the sky, which gently move, ripple and change. They are usually greenish, but can sometimes be white, blue, purple or red.

North and south

These displays of shimmering light are called the *aurora borealis*, or Northern lights, and the *aurora australis*, or Southern lights. They appear around the North and South poles, so you can usually only see them if you are quite far north or south.

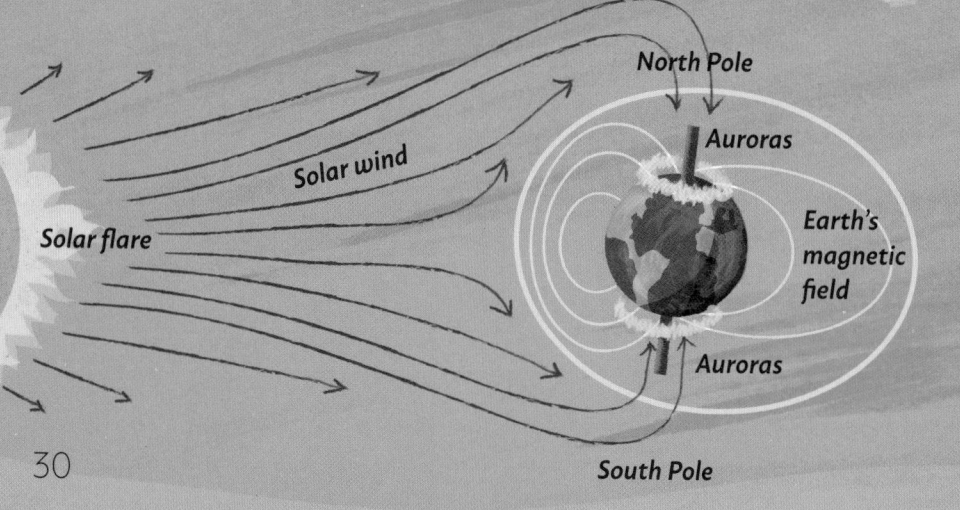

North Pole

Auroras

Solar wind

Earth's magnetic field

Solar flare

Auroras

South Pole

How do they work?

The auroras are caused by sudden explosions of energy on the Sun. They throw out a "solar wind" of electrically charged particles, which fly out into space. As the particles approach Earth, the Earth's magnetic field channels them towards the poles. The charged particles crash into oxygen and nitrogen gas in the Earth's atmosphere, making it glow. The different colours depend on which type of gas is glowing, and how high above the Earth's surface it is.

Aurora stories

There are all kinds of folktales and ancient beliefs about auroras. For some Inuit peoples, the Northern lights were the spirits of those who had died, dancing, playing or waving to the living at night. In Finnish folklore, the aurora is the *revontulet*, or "fox fires", caused by the mythical Fire Fox running across the north and sweeping snow and sparks up into the sky with his tail. Some Aboriginal people of southern Australia saw the Southern lights as the campfires of spirits or ghosts in the land of the dead.

SEEING AN AURORA

How can you see an aurora? One way is to travel to somewhere in the far north or south of the world. Lots of travel companies run special tourist trips and holidays especially to see them. Sometimes, when the Sun is very active, a big release of particles can make an extra-large aurora that is visible further away from the poles. If this happens, there are usually news stories about it, telling you when to watch out for it.